D0463256

DATE DUE

DEC 02

JUN 13 05			
GAYLORD			PRINTED IN U.S.A.

SEASONS of the CIRCLE
A Native American Year

by Joseph Bruchac / illustrated by Robert F. Goetzl

Troll

JACKSON COUNTY LIBRARY SERVICES
MEDFORD, OREGON 97501

For Bonita and all the other members of the Rainbow of Strength Abenaki Children's Dance Troupe—your feet are following the circle.
—J.B.

For my family and friends, whose love encourages and sustains me.
—R.G.

ACKNOWLEDGMENTS

The author and illustrator would like to extend special thanks to the following people who generously provided helpful information: Herman Agoyo; Alan Caldwell, Menominee Indian Tribe of Wisconsin; Elgin Crows Breast, Cultural Preservation Office, Fort Berthold Tribal Business Council; Michael Lapaca; Roger Paul, Director of Language, and Brian Reynolds, Education Director, Houlton Band of Maliseet Indians; and Bo Taylor, Archivist, Museum of the Cherokee Indian.

Text copyright © 2002 by Joseph Bruchac.

Illustrations copyright © 2002 by Robert F. Goetzl.

Published by BridgeWater Books, an imprint and registered trademark of Troll Communications L.L.C.

All rights reserved. No part of this book may be reproduced or utilized in any form or by any means, electronic or mechanical, including photocopying, recording, or by any information storage and retrieval system, without written permission from the publisher.

Printed in Singapore.

10 9 8 7 6 5 4 3 2 1

Library of Congress Cataloging-in-Publication Data

Bruchac, Joseph, 1942–
    Seasons of the circle : a Native American year / written by Joseph Bruchac ; illustrated by Robert F. Goetzl.
      p.   cm.
    Summary: Illustrations and brief text introduce activities of various Native American people in each month of the year.
    ISBN 0-8167-7467-6
    1. Indians of North America—Social life and customs—Juvenile literature.
    2. Seasons—Juvenile literature. [1. Indians of North America—Social life and customs.
    2. Months. 3. Seasons.] I. Goetzl, Robert F., ill. II. Title.

E98.S7 B78 2002
391'.0089'97—dc21   2002020013

AUTHOR'S NOTE

More than four hundred different American Indian tribal nations can be found in what is now the United States. Although their languages, traditional customs, and ways of life vary greatly, all American Indian peoples have a number of things in common.

One of those things is the concept of the circle. The circle is a sacred shape. It reminds us that all things are interconnected. It teaches us that our lives move in circles rather than along a straight line. That which happened once may happen again.

The seasons move in a great circle, too, returning again and again from one year to the next. The activities that people engage in through that circle of the seasons are also repeated, each done at its proper time. This remains just as true today as it was five hundred years ago. Hunting, fishing, gathering food, ceremonies of celebration and thanksgiving, rites of passage, and the making of traditional crafts are among the many activities that remain linked to the cycle of seasons for Native Americans.

In some cases, these practices have been modified to include new ideas or technology introduced by the newcomers who began arriving on North American shores five centuries ago. In the Southwest, for example, the feast days of the Catholic saints have become a public part of Pueblo ceremonies. A basketmaker among the O'odham may use a steel needle, or a Cherokee berry picker may use a plastic bucket while gathering the annual harvest of strawberries. However, the old cycle has not changed—the seasons of the circle remain the same. So it is that some of the activities in this book are shown as they were long ago and others appear as they are today.

Just as the old circle remains, so too Native people are still here. Contemporary Native Americans are found all over the United States and Canada, in every modern profession, and they are important parts of the patchwork quilt that is multicultural America. But a great many of them return to their tribal nations each year to take part in ceremonies and traditional activities when the turning seasons call them home.

This simple book depicts only a handful of contemporary Native tribal nations. The people and the activities they are engaged in have been chosen to represent the broad sweep of the many regions of this continent. We hope that this small sampling will lead you to look further along the circle. You can start by looking at the website for the National Museum of the American Indian (**www.nmai.si.edu**). To learn more about native cultures and to find links to many tribal nations visit **www.nativeculture.com/lisamitten/nations.html**.

JANUARY

Maliseet hunters follow
the tracks of the moose
through crusted snow.

FEBRUARY

Along the surface of a frozen lake

Mohawk men and boys play

the game of snow snake.

MARCH

As the snow starts to melt

and the nights still freeze

Lenape women gather sap,

a sweet gift from the maple trees.

APRIL

When the Moon of Ice Breaking is reborn
Hidatsa farmers along the Missouri
plant seeds for beans, squash, and corn.

MAY

Cherokee people gather berries where
the warmth of Grandmother Sun has touched,
reminding them sweetness was meant to share.

JUNE

At the annual feast days for St. John
San Juan Pueblo boys and girls run
to greet the dawn.

JULY

Mountain Spirit Dancers
circle the fire again
to honor an Apache girl
who has now become a woman.

AUGUST

Suquamish men and women race
in their dugout canoes
during Chief Seattle Days.

SEPTEMBER

A Menominee wild rice harvester
slowly poles his canoe
through still green water.

OCTOBER

With yucca, bear grass, and i'huk seeds
an O'odham woman weaves
a basket in patterns learned from a dream.

NOVEMBER

Havasupai men build a winter home,

its door open to the blessing of the rising sun.

DECEMBER
In the Moon When Wolves Run Together,
in a buffalo-skin tipi, a Lakota elder
tells stories of when earth was young.

MEANING AND PRONUNCIATION OF TRIBAL NAMES

Today, the names commonly accepted for many American Indian tribal nations are not the names those nations originally used. Sometimes the eastern Native American nations called the nations farther to the west by different names than those nations called themselves. When the European newcomers first arrived, they met members of the eastern nations and learned the names that these nations used. It is those names that have endured over time. In other cases, the Europeans gave entirely new names to Native people. All of the tribal names mentioned in this book are accepted today by the Native people to which they refer. Here are brief descriptions of each Native tribe in this book. The map on pages 30–31 indicates where each tribe was originally located in North America.

CHEROKEE: (Chair'-oh-key) *Tennessee, Kentucky, North Carolina, South Carolina, and Georgia.* Their name for themselves is *Aniyunwiya* (ah-ni-yoon-wee'-yah), which means "Principal People" or "Real People." *Cherokee* is the anglicized form of *Tsalagi* (Chah'-lah-gee), which some believe came from a Choctaw word meaning "people of the cave country." Early in the nineteenth century, the great majority of Cherokees were removed from the South to Oklahoma on the Trail of Tears. The Cherokees survived to become the largest American Indian tribal nation. The Cherokee Nation of Oklahoma has 308,000 members, while the Eastern Cherokees, who live in North Carolina, number over 9,000.

HAVASUPAI: (Hah-vah-su'-pie) *Arizona.* These are the people who live at the bottom of the Grand Canyon in Arizona. The reservation can be reached only by helicopter, on horse, or by foot trails. "People Who Live at the Place Which Is Green" is the literal translation of their name. In the spring and summer, crops were traditionally grown in the canyon, but in the autumn the tribe would move to winter villages on the plateau to hunt. Today, more than thirty thousand tourists visit the Havasupai community every year, so you would probably have to make a reservation to visit their reservation!

HIDATSA: (He-daht'-sah) *North Dakota.* Known as the merchants and farmers of the northern plains, the Hidatsa lived in permanent earth-lodge villages where the Knife River joins the Missouri River in present-day North Dakota. Today, their main reservation, which they share with the Mandan (Man'-dan) and Arikara (Ah-ri'-kah-rah) tribes, is at Fort Berthold, close to their old home.

LAKOTA: (Lah-ko'-tah) *North Dakota, South Dakota, Nebraska, and Montana.* The Lakota are the people of the Great Plains, and they are known to many as the *Sioux* (probably derived from a Chippewa word meaning "snakes"). The Lakota are known as hunters of the buffalo and fierce defenders of their homeland, and their way of life and clothing have become the popular image of the American Indian. Sitting Bull and Crazy Horse were famous Lakota warriors.

LENAPE: (Leh-nah'-pay) *Southeastern New York, New Jersey, Delaware, and Eastern Pennsylvania.* The name *Lenape* means "Real People." Traditionally, the Lenape Nation lived along the Delaware River. In the early colonial period, Europeans began calling the Lenape people the Delawares, and great pressure was put on the Lenapes to sell their land and move west. Today, small, loosely organized communities of Lenape people still exist in New Jersey and Pennsylvania. Other Delawares can be found in Ontario among the Iroquois and in Oklahoma, where the Delaware Nation lives in the midst of the Cherokees.

MALISEET: (Mah'-leh-seet) *New Brunswick (Canada) and Northern Maine.* Along with the closely related Passamaquoddys (Pass-ah-mah-kwah'-dee), Micmacs (Mik'-mak), Penobscots (Peh-nahb'-scaht), and Western Abenakis (Ah-beh-nah'-kee), the Maliseet are part of the Wabanaki (Wah-beh-nah'-kee), or "Dawn Land," Confederacy. *Maliseet* appears to come from a Micmac word meaning "lazy speakers." Their original name for themselves is *Wawlastawkwiyak* (Waa-lah-tawk'-wee-yak), the "People of the Beautiful River," referring to the St. John's River.

MENOMINEE: (Meh'-no-meh-ne) *Northern Wisconsin along Lake Michigan.* The name *Menominee* translates as "Wild Rice People." Terminated as a tribe by the U.S. government in the 1950s, the Menominee fought successfully to regain recognition and are now a thriving community living in the heart of the old homeland in a densely forested part of northeast Wisconsin.

MOHAWK: (Mo'-hawk) *New York State.* One of the original five Nations of the Iroquois Confederacy, the Mohawk call themselves *Ganienkehgaono* (Gah-nyen-keh'-gah-oh-no), or "People of the Flint." Their original villages, made of huge elm-bark longhouses, were along the eastern part of the Mohawk River. In recent years, Mohawk men have gained a reputation as fearless steel workers building tall skyscrapers. Present-day Mohawk reservations exist in both Canada and northern New York.

O'ODHAM: (Oh'-ohd-hum) *Sonoran Mexico and southern Arizona, especially in the desert areas south of present-day Tucson.* The Tohono O'odham are often referred to as the *Papago*, a name coming from *pappah*, their word for beans. *O'odham* means "The People." Beans, corn, and cotton were their primary crops, which they grew using a sophisticated system of irrigation. Today, they still harvest many wild plants from the desert. O'odham women are well-known for their basketry.

SAN JUAN PUEBLO: (San wahn') *New Mexico.* San Juan Pueblo is one of the numerous Pueblo communities whose towns in New Mexico are found close to the Rio Grande River. The people of San Juan, just south of Santa Fe, speak the *Tewa* (Tay'-wah) language and are the largest population of the Tewa Pueblos. Expert agriculturalists, the people of San Juan developed sophisticated irrigation systems, using canals, dams, and ditches, long before the coming of Europeans. The artists of San Juan are famous today for their colorful pottery and have their own Oke Oweenge Arts and Crafts Cooperative.

SUQUAMISH: (Sue-kwah'-mish) *Coastal Washington.* The great wooden longhouses of the Suquamish people around Puget Sound were home to a nation of seagoing fishermen. Today, the Suquamish still live close to Puget Sound. They are probably best known for one of their most famous and eloquent chiefs, Chief Seattle, for whom nearby Seattle, Washington, was named.

WHITE MOUNTAIN APACHE: (Ah-pah'-chee) *Eastern Arizona.* The name *Apache* appears to come from a Zuñi word meaning "enemies." The Apache call themselves *Tindeh* (Tin-dey'), meaning "The People." Before the arrival of Europeans, the Apache lived a very mobile existence, building brush shelters and moving seasonally to hunt and harvest wild foods. Their resistance to Spanish and New Mexican slave raiders and later to the U.S. Army gained them a reputation as fierce guerrilla warriors. Today, their spectacularly scenic reservation, where the Apaches operate a ski resort and the White Mountain Apache Motel, is a favorite tourist destination.

SUBARCTIC

NORTHWEST
COAST

Suquamish—

PLATEAU

Hidatsa

Lakota

Lakota

GREAT
BASIN

PLAINS

CALIFORNIA

Havasupai

White
Mountain
Apache

San Juan
Pueblo

O'odham

SOUTH

WEST

Maliseet

Menominee

Mohawk

Lenape

Lenape

EASTERN
WOODLANDS

Lenape

Cherokee   Cherokee

Cherokee

NOTE

Scholars have divided
North America into eight
"tribal regions." The tribes
in each region have many
cultural and economic
similarities, and they share
many of the same traditions.
The tribal nations mentioned
in this book come from the
four corners of North America,
and they represent four of
the tribal regions.

MOON NAMES

The great majority of Native American tribal nations kept track of the seasons by giving names to each of the full moons during the year. Each moon name was chosen to reflect natural events happening at that time of year. Today, those moon names correspond to the twelve months of the calendar year. The names often differ greatly from one part of the country to another. The chart shows examples of moon names from three tribes.

	MOHAWKS (Northeast)	LAKOTAS (Great Plains)	SUQUAMISH (Northwest)
JANUARY	Coldest Moon	Moon of Popping Trees	Younger Brother
FEBRUARY	Days Starting to Lengthen Moon	Sore Eyes Moon	Blowing or Windy
MARCH	Moon of More Sunlight	Moon When Grass Comes Up	Frog Face
APRIL	Trees Budding Moon	Moon When Buffalo Calves Are Born	Bird Whistling
MAY	Full Leaf Moon	Thunderstorm Moon	Digging Camas Bulbs
JUNE	Fruits Ripening Moon	Ripe Berries Moon	Salmonberries
JULY	Moon When Everything Is Ripe	Chokecherry Moon	Blackberries
AUGUST	Harvest Moon	Moon of Wild Plums	Salalberries
SEPTEMBER	Moon When Leaves Are No Longer Green	Yellow Leaves Moon	Silver Salmon
OCTOBER	Moon of Hard Times Starting	Moon of Leaves Falling	Dog Salmon
NOVEMBER	Snow Coming Moon	Moon When the Buffalo Calves Lose Their Hair	Put Your Canoe Paddles Away
DECEMBER	Moon of Freezing	Moon When Wolves Run Together	Older Brother